Think Yourself Happy

Happiness Is Yours

Karen Echols - Green

Kingdom Trailblazers Publishing

KINGDOM TRAILBLAZERS
Publishing

This book is dedicated to my devoted husband, my children, my loving mother, TT Robbie, James Smith (author, mentor, and my former Sunday school teacher), and everyone who has inspired me in some way along my journey in life.

Table of Contents

Keep the Joy

The glory of this latter house shall be greater than of the former, saith the Lord of hosts: and in this place will I give peace, saith the Lord of hosts.
Haggai 2:9 KJV

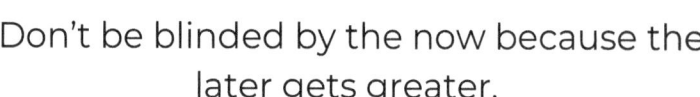

Don't be blinded by the now because the later gets greater.

When you reach a stumbling block, don't let it stop you. Build on it instead, because you already have the foundation, and this is what endures.

When you are feeling down, start thinking happy thoughts about what God has done for you. This will help you to quickly halt the negative thoughts and realize that you have no reason or need to stay in that place.

Think happy thoughts and get to your happy place. Keep your joy and give your troubles to God.

Be kind: you might change someone's life, and you might gain a friend.

Never let anyone take the "joy" out of your day. Don't give them that much power over you.

Sometimes you must make yourself do things, even when you feel you can't, to get to where you need to be.

Out of poverty, great people stand. They become what they were meant to be because they didn't let their present circumstances dictate their outcome.

Be positive, see positive, and embrace positivity in all that you do.

You've got what it takes, so take what you have and do what you need to get to where you want to go. Get to it!

Stay Strong

What time I am afraid, I will trust in thee. In God I will praise his word, in God I have put my trust; I will not fear what flesh can do unto me.

Psalm 56: 3-4 KJV

Have you ever felt deeply distressed when you come to a crossroad in your life and must make that decision? It can happen at any point in your life, at any stage, at any age, and at many times over and over again.

Sometimes you never seem to know where to cross. Just walk and trust God: He will meet you at every turn.

Find the light whenever you're going through a difficult time. The metaphor "there is light at the end of the tunnel" is true. Just keep walking, run if you must, until you find your way out.

Negativity detracts from your moral character and stops you from reaching your true potential.

Stay true to you and never change for anyone, because who are they but another you: a sinner saved by grace. The true change should be for God.

There is a common saying that a mind is a terrible thing to waste and it's true. The mind is guided by the heart, and your heart is the soul of your mind, so guard your heart in everything you do.

Egos can be too big. Don't let your ego become so inflated that it stops you from soaring to your highest potential. Whatever it is, let it go, so you can continue to grow.

Each day brings a new opportunity to change the next day.

Author Jim Lawson has stated, 'If you don't have a seat at the table, bring a folding chair.' I say, stand if you have to, so you can be seen and heard.

A few ingredients to build and sustain a well-rounded life: stay humble, stay grounded, and stay rooted.

Don't look back at what you have lost or left behind. Instead, look ahead to the exciting things that are about to happen in your life.

Love is The Key

But God commendeth his love toward us, in that, while we were yet sinners, Christ died for us.
Romans 5:8 KJV

We have an overflow of abundance of love and there is no price on it. It is something that cannot be purchased but is freely given to you from God through the love of Jesus Christ.

So there shouldn't be any reason why you can't give it freely. Give love and it shall be given back to you.

Love can't be bought, love can't be bargained, love can't be gambled, love can't be compromised, love can't be reasoned, love can't be stolen. Love can only be given.

You will have more joy if you love more and judge less.

God commanded us not to judge, but to love.

The main goal for everyone, no matter their walk of life, is to love more, give more, and be a blessing to others. This is following God's way of life.

Forgiveness is very powerful, but it is one of the most difficult things to do. We must always bear in mind that we are living today because God has forgiven us through Jesus Christ.

When you forgive, you take back your own power. Simply think about Jesus Christ and what he did for our forgiveness to take place.

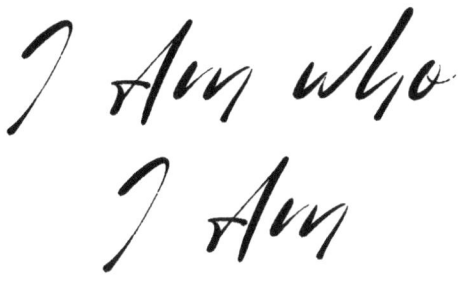

I Am who
I Am

For I know the thoughts that I think toward you, saith the Lord, thoughts of peace, and not of evil, to give you an expected end.
Jeremiah 29:11 KJV

You are the only one who can live out your purpose. Don't think about it, just live it.

I am who God says I am, not who man makes me up to be according to his opinion.

You don't need to do anything important to be important. You are important because God made you so that's important enough to just be you!

Look within to win because the winner is in you!

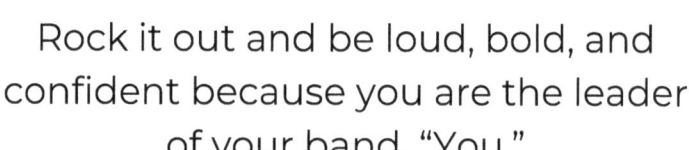

Rock it out and be loud, bold, and confident because you are the leader of your band, "You."

You are uniquely made so be the best YOU that you were designed to be.

You are who you think you are, so think awesome!

We spend too much time thinking outside of ourselves but your peace and whole being comes from within you: only you can bring that out.

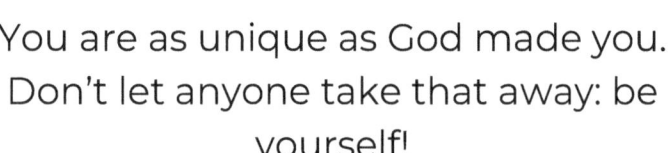

You are as unique as God made you. Don't let anyone take that away: be yourself!

Be your unique self and live your life as God planned: the world needs you.

Let's be humble and pray. Lord, please help me to be the 'me' that you want me to be.

Have you ever thought about the meaning of the phrase: "to thine own self be true?"

I have, and when I see it on bumper stickers and read it somewhere in a book, I always wonder about it. I think I know the meaning now, and it's simple: you are you, and only you truly know yourself.

People can guess and say who and what they think you are, but ultimately, you are the only one that knows–and of course, our Heavenly Father.

So always be true to yourself because you know your capabilities.

Happiness is Yours

Now the God of hope fill you with all joy and peace in believing, that ye may abound in hope, through the power of the Holy Ghost.
Romans 15:13 KJV

Happiness is meant for everyone to have in abundance. We are creatures of habit and change can be difficult, and not always what we want to do.

I have realized that you must change sometimes to be able to move on, to find your happiness, and to be at peace. We already know what we need to do but it's the act of not doing so that holds us back. Just do it!

I know it is easy to say, but I guarantee if you start practicing and living it, you will see it becomes easier and easier to do.

Find your happy place and be comfortable with who you are becoming daily.

My five key things to a happy life: keep loving, keep giving, keep achieving, keep dreaming, and keep forgiving!

I was listening to an actor on a late-night show who said something that stuck with me. He went on to say, "DDHD." Everyone looked amazed and wondered what it meant. He explained, "Dreams don't have deadlines."

This is a great expression, and it's true, so go ahead, go after those dreams!

You can change your tomorrow by preparing for it today.

You are destined to be great; don't wait, it's your time to shine.

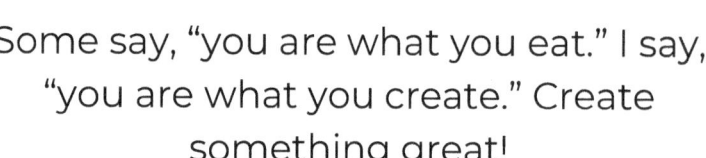

Some say, "you are what you eat." I say, "you are what you create." Create something great!

For most of my life, I thought that happiness came from having lots of money and friends. Well, I have found out that neither is true. Happiness comes from within.

The Delight of the Lord

Delight thyself also in the Lord; and He shall give thee the desires of thine heart.

Psalm 37:4 KJV

When people say, "life is full of surprises," I think they are right. I like to say: be prepared for anything, because God's blessings may come at any time and hit you suddenly, like lightning. Don't be caught off-guard, because if you prayed for it, be prepared to receive it.

God's word stands true, and He will give you the desires of your heart: but you must align yourself up with Him. So "delight yourself in the Lord."

What gives you your fight to keep going? Is it people? People will leave you. Is it money? Money doesn't last. Is it material things? Material things fade away. Stand by the word and promises of God; He will never leave you, nor forsake you.

To be able to live a life of service to others is the greatest responsibility of anyone's story.

Forgiveness is free: always be open to forgive to take that burden off you.

Walk in your faith, walk in your courage, walk in your strength: it's there, and you have it.

Stay true to you for you, love you for you, and always let God lead you.

Each day brings so many great possibilities. Simply focus your mind and you can tap into them.

The Lord is the source of my daily strength, the strength on which I stand. I cannot stand without Him.

When I was very young and growing up, my mom had a small plaque hanging in the hallway of our home with the Serenity Prayer engraved on it in gold lettering.

It read:
"God grant me the serenity to accept the things that I cannot change, the courage to change the things that I can, and the wisdom to know the difference."

I didn't know how profound the words on that plaque were until I was old enough to understand it.

It simply means to trust God in everything to give you peace and calmness when you need it, give you courage at the very moment you need it, and to bless you with wisdom to make the right choices.

What's my Purpose

He hath shewed thee, O man, what is good; and what doth the Lord require of thee, but to do justly, and to love mercy, and to walk humbly with thy God.

Micah 6:8

You were made for a purpose and life becomes more fulfilling when you find that purpose. Look and seek for your purpose by continuing to pray and ask God for guidance.

This will lead you to become a bigger and better person who can contribute to this society more than you will ever imagine. Only you can be you, and only you can live out your purpose.

Do today what you know will last and have meaning and purpose for tomorrow.

Just remember: if you are still breathing, you still have a purpose.

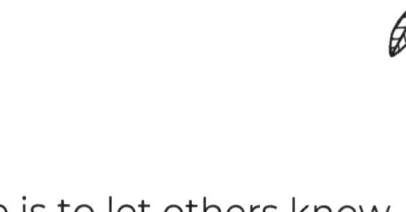

Our daily purpose is to let others know
that God is, God can, and God will.

Make your mission your purpose and
your purpose your mission.

I have always questioned, "what's my purpose in life?" Some people have spent lots of money seeking to find their purpose in life and some have been successful in their quest.

I believe you already have within you what you need to find and live out your purpose, because God has provided each of us with the power to consciously go in the appropriate direction.

We sometimes need a little inspiration (or *mustard seed faith*) to get us there.

Some may ask, "why write a book of inspiration?" and I answer, "why not?" God has placed something in everyone, and for me, He instilled a passion for writing to encourage, inspire, and motivate others.

We live in a world where there are so many negative things. We must always be armed with the power to overcome and withstand our trials and tribulations.

Sometimes just a short positive phrase, an inspirational note, or a brief Bible verse is all we need to keep going.

Smile and Be Happy

Rejoice in the Lord always: and again I say, Rejoice.
Philippians 4:4

Look at life like a party: celebrate often!

Ask God for favor because favor is the savor (sweetness) of life and favor ain't fair but it sho' is good!

Life is short: make your days happy. Smile, laugh, rejoice, celebrate, and boy oh boy, enjoy!

Have your heard "find your why?" Why do you do what you do every day? You should wake up with every thought focused on the "why" the Lord has given you another day. It is surely not to be spent angry, upset, mean, unhappy, and ungrateful.

Don't waste the time God has given you. Smile, be happy, and make a positive difference in someone else's life.

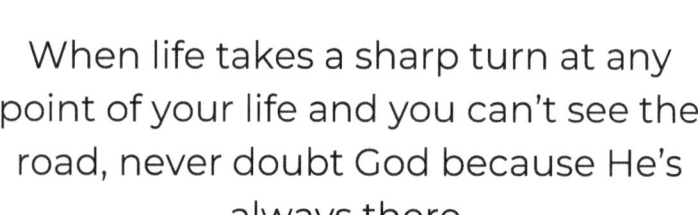

When life takes a sharp turn at any point of your life and you can't see the road, never doubt God because He's always there.

Inspire yourself to be yourself.

Make this day your day because you own it.

Keep Going

And let us not be weary in well doing: for in due season we shall reap, if we faint not.
Galatians 6:9

No one can make anything happen for you, but YOU!

We are constantly in a process of transformation to become what God has planned for us to be. However, we must free our minds and hearts to accept that change.

If you doubt yourself, who will believe in you?

Always think victory, never defeat!

God always has something in the making for you. Keep the faith and keep trying because life is good.

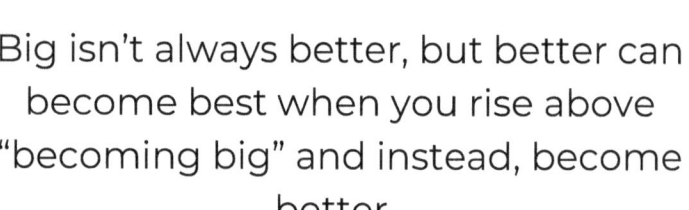

Big isn't always better, but better can become best when you rise above "becoming big" and instead, become better.

We sometimes say people get a second chance, but honestly, everyday offers new chances.

Have you ever felt as though you let your ego get in the way of the biggest opportunity you may have ever had? You are not alone if you have, because it has happened to most of us.

Next time, take yourself out of it and look ahead to what the opportunity will lead to, not your present state. After all, it's just the beginning–stay in it until the end.

You are better today than yesterday because you are closer to your dreams. And God is always with you, more than it may seem. Just keep going!

It doesn't matter where you start, it's in where you finish. You truly start all over again every morning with every breath you take. God gives you a fresh new start to try again. So, take a deep breath, exhale, and start over!

Stay Tuned into God

Unto thee, O Lord, do I lift up my soul. O my God, I trust in thee: let me not be ashamed, let not mine enemies triumph over me.
Psalm 25: 1-2 KJV

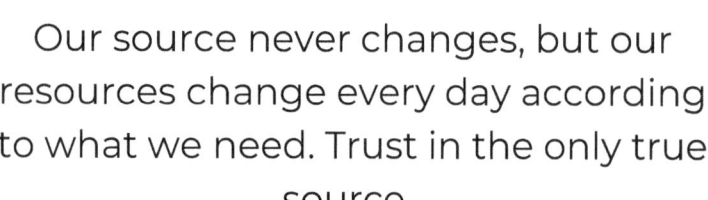

Our source never changes, but our resources change every day according to what we need. Trust in the only true source.

Never fret, never fear, never give up, and never give in, because with God, you will always win.

God wants us, yet most of our lives we run after people who don't want us. So, you are much better served to seek God: the one who wants you. He's your best choice!

If you are going to trust and believe God, let Him be God in your life.

Hold out through the night, in the morning God will make it alright.

I often tell my children to do or become what they want to do or become. For example, if you aspire to be a doctor or an artist, and have the talent and aptitude to do so, then take that path.

Sometimes, we get on a wrong path and stay on it for too long. You can always find your path, but you need to know for yourself that it's the right one. This is where and when you take the time for YOU to find out.

Thank God for grace and mercy. Without it, we would be clueless, and let's be honest: we would simply be lost.

Some say, "No problem is too hard for God." I say, it is if you don't take it to the Lord and leave it there.

Life is about becoming who God created you to be. If you have not yet become what you were created to be, then it is your goal to seek and achieve what you were created to become.

Our focus on God includes:

F: Forgiving others as Christ would.
O: Obedience to God's word.
C: Compassion by bearing the pain of others.
U: Understanding of others and do not judge.
S: Serve others as God has instructed us.

To grow spiritually through God, you must have focus.

In the game of sports, one team must lose for the other to win. But in Christ, we are all winners–get on His team.

You have the power within you to overcome any obstacle, sometimes you must pull from a higher power (God) to uncover that strength.

Be Blessed

Blessed be the God and Father of our Lord Jesus Christ, who hath blessed us with all spiritual blessings in heavenly places in Christ.

Ephesians 1:3

God will bless you in the moment, for the moment, and when there are no moments left.

Always remember, my blessings are my blessings, and your blessings are your blessings. God will never cross our blessings.

People will only respect you as much as you respect yourself.

Start using your talent and energy in positive spaces that matter every day, why waste it?

Think beyond what you feel you can't do.

Dream your dream but be sure to put your dream into action so it can come true for you. Only you can make your dream a reality.

Give it or take it, leave it or make it: the choice is yours.

Be ready for God's unexpected blessings and stand on solid ground, because when one comes along, it may knock you off your feet.

Life is full of possibilities as well as challenges. Don't let your challenges keep you where you are.

The possibilities will lead you to the road of success, but first you must work through your challenges to reach those possibilities and succeed.

Live your Life

As every man hath received the gift, even so minister the same one to another, as good stewards of the manifold grace of God.

1 Peter 4:10

While living, make life worth living and be a blessing to someone else.

Life is good when you let it be. Open up to what is good and right in your life and celebrate it all.

Life is uncertain at times but it's not for you to worry about or try to figure out. God has already paved the way for you and the path is straight.

Don't stop living trying to figure life out. Precious time has already been wasted on thinking, when you should be living!

Life is short and sweet, so savor every moment, because in time it will be gone.

Turn your "I can" attitude into an "I will" attitude. Yes, you can do it—but will you?

Capture life in the moment before it passes by, because every moment is one that will never pass your way again.

Don't measure yourself by the gifts God has given others: remember the gifts that God has given you and you will always measure up.

Life has a way of knocking you off track, but don't stay on the sidelines. Get back up and run your race as fast as you can until you reach victory.

God has instilled different gifts within each of us. I can only perform mine and you, yours. We spend a lot of time trying to be someone else and if you live someone else's life, who's going to live yours?

Author's Favorite Scriptures

For I know the thoughts that I think toward you, saith the Lord, thoughts of peace, and not of evil, to give you an expected end.
Jeremiah 29:11 KJV

I can do all things through Christ who strengthens me.
Philippians 4:13 KJV

About the Author

Karen Echols-Green is a high school graduate of Coldwater High School in Coldwater, MS. She also graduated from Northwest MS Jr College with an AA Degree in Mass Communication and the University of Southern MS with a BS Degree in Radio, Television, and Film with a Minor in Journalism.

She has been in leadership for over 30 years, coaching and developing skills and professional growth for Customer Service Teams. She's an avid runner with over fifty marathons and half marathons combined that she has completed and is still running. She runs to support charities and help them raise money for their missions.

Her passion has been encouraging people to know their worth and be the best version of themselves. She often states, "*no one can be you but you.*" Her favorite motivational saying is: *Favor ain't fair, but it sho' is good! And Life is good, celebrate!* She writes to encourage, motivate, and inspire others.